Revised Edition

The Compelling Christ

Why We Can Be Sure of the Bible, Christ, and Salvation

Floyd C. McElveen

Institute for Religious Research
Grand Rapids, Michigan 49505

Copyright © 1989, 1991 by Floyd C. McElveen

The Institute for Religious Research is
the research and publishing division of
Gospel Truths Ministries,
1340 Monroe, N.W.,
Grand Rapids, MI 49505-4622.

Scripture quotations are from the
King James Version
unless otherwise designated.

ISBN 0-9620963-1-8

CONTENTS

Introduction 4

1 Compelling Evidence 6

2 Salvation: Clear and Biblical 30

3 The Christ Changed Life 41

Introduction

Many who read this book may not be familiar with the basic message of the Bible. For this reason, we include a very brief summary of God's plan for mankind as recorded in the Bible, God's proven source book. These Bible facts along with chapter two of this book may enable the reader to make an intelligent decision to personally receive the Lord Jesus Christ.

The Bible teaches that in the beginning God created the heavens and the earth. . . . He created every living thing. . . . In the day that He created man, He made him in the image and likeness of God. He created them male and female, and blessed them. Then God saw everything that He had made and He pronounced it very good.

However, the Scriptural record goes on to explain that the first man and woman, Adam and Eve, were tempted by the fallen angelic being, Satan, and chose to disobey God. Through this sin they fell from their original state of innocence and were cut off from the fellowship they had enjoyed with a holy God. They died spiritually; physical death followed.

Everything changed at this point. This fall affected the whole human race. A sin nature replaced man's former innocence, and all creation came under the judgement of God.

However, though the human race was now separated from the Creator, God in His love made a provision for man's redemption from the power of sin and death through His Son, Jesus Christ. God's plan as it is gradually unfolded in the Bible, involved the preparation of a special people through whom He revealed His Word so that man may know the true way. In due time God sent His Son, the Messiah, to die in our place and pay the penalty for our sins that God's perfect justice demanded. Two thousand years ago Jesus Christ was crucified, died, and buried. His shed blood on the cross was the atonement for the sins of mankind. His resurrection demonstrated that He was no mere man, but God come in the flesh.

The Scriptures state that salvation is a free gift for those who will accept Christ's death as the complete provision for their forgiveness and reconciliation to God. Christ has assured us that He will come again for His own. Those who have received Him by faith will live with Christ forever and those who reject Him will be separated to everlasting punishment.

Perhaps you question whether the Bible really is the revealed Word of God, as it claims to be. If so, please read chapter one carefully. It presents compelling evidence for the trustworthiness of the Bible.

1

Compelling Evidence

"The Bible must be the invention of either good men or angels, bad men or devils, or of God. (1) It could not be the invention of good men or angels, for they neither would or could make a book, and tell lies all the time they were writing it, saying, 'Thus saith the Lord,' when it was their own invention. (2) It could not be the invention of bad men or devils, for they would not make a book which commands all duty, forbids all sin, and condemns their souls to hell for all eternity. (3) Therefore I draw this conclusion, that the Bible must be given by divine inspiration"(Charles Wesley).

I suspect all of us have a "Bible" by which we live, whether we are aware of it or not. The "Bible" I personally lived by was a mishmash of my own wisdom and that of others. These sources—books, sometimes famous scientists, psychologists, professors and my own conclusions—often were uncertain, prone to error, and speculative. All of the sources for my "Bible" were cluttered with mistakes and full of naked opinions. My "Bible" was unsure about the origin and purpose of life and man's destiny. If this is true of others also, my heart cries out for my fellow travellers on the road of life. In the love of one who is now my Saviour, I ask, "Is this true of your 'Bible'? Have the sources you may be depending on ever made mistakes? Do they have final and absolute knowledge? Do you? Will you risk your life, your eternal destiny, on wishful thinking or opinions?" Dear reader, you and I know this is not the measure of truth.

By contrast, the Christian's Bible is God's Word—certain, infallible and proven in a thousand battles.

The Bible claims to be the Word of God. Some 3,800 times, phrases including "Thus saith the Lord," "The Word of the Lord came to me," and others express these claims. 2 Timothy 3:16, for example, tells us that, "All scripture is given by inspiration of God, and is profitable for doctrine, for reproof, for correction, for instruction in righteousness."

Consider a number of key areas in which the Bible has proven itself reliable. Each of these proofs is impressive, but together they provide unshakable evidence for its authority as the revealed Word of God.

Unity

Imagine forty men, separated in time by centuries, coming from many different cultures, towns, cities, and backgrounds. Imagine that they are working independently on a statue of Jesus. Each has a particular part of the statue to carve: one, a toe; one, an ear; another, the neck; another, the chin; another, a leg; yet another, a shoulder blade; and so on. After hundreds of years, all of these carvings are brought to one place and put together. Incredibly, they all fit together perfectly, and form a beautiful statue of Jesus. Impossible, by chance. Possible only by the superintending act of a supervising God.

Yet this is exactly what we have in the writing of the Bible. Some forty authors, working over a period of nearly 1,600 years, writing sixty-six books, came up with a perfectly unified book portraying one perfect person—the Lord Jesus Christ!

Archaeology

More than 25,000 sites have been excavated verifying the existence of cities, kings, kingdoms, events, officials, etc. proving the historicity and incredible accuracy of thousands of Biblical references. Archaeologist Nelson Glueck has said, "It may be stated categorically that no archaeological discovery has ever controverted a biblical reference."

Fantastic!... in a book thousands of years old! *Since we can trust the Bible in the things we can see, we know we can trust it in the things we cannot see.*

Science

Although skeptics have claimed that the Bible contains scientific errors, none of the allegations have been proven. This is true of no other ancient religious book. In fact, many times science has been proven wrong and the Bible right. Science textbooks are changed frequently and often hopelessly contradict one another after a few years. The Bible never has to be changed. It is accurate where it touches on science. For example, in a day when most people thought the earth was flat, even up to the voyage of Columbus in 1492, the Bible stated in Isaiah 40:22a, "It is he that sitteth upon the *circle* of the earth." The word for "circle" is the Hebrew word meaning "round" or "sphere". In other words, the Bible revealed that the earth was a sphere about 2,200 years before man found it out, even though Marco Polo had made some strides in that direction a few centuries before Columbus. But Isaiah wrote about 700 years B. C.! How did Isaiah know? He didn't, the word came from God!

The Jews

Deuteronomy 28:25, 26 tells us of the future suffering and scattering of the Jews, and Deuteronomy 30:1-6 adds to this prophecy, which had indicated that the Jews would be scattered among all nations, but would someday be regathered to their own land. These prophecies were given centuries before the fulfillment. Yet God had given very literal prophecies concerning the inheritance of the land of Palestine to Abraham and to the Jews. Leviticus 26:31-33, given about 1400 B.C. adds to this prophecy, as does Ezekiel 36:33-35 and Ezekiel 37. Luke 21:23, 24 reasserts these prophecies. It was also predicted that Jerusalem would be trampled underfoot by the Gentiles until the time of the Gentiles is fulfilled.

From these and other Scriptures let us give a brief summary of what God's Word says the future held for the Jews. (1) Scattering, worldwide among all nations. (2) Intense persecution and suffering. (3) Other, mightier nations around them would be destroyed, but they would never lose their identity as Jews, and a remnant would always survive. (4) They would someday return to their own land and reestablish their own nation.

Now consider these well known facts. The Jews were surrounded by formidable and warlike people, some of them more numerous and more powerful than the Jews. Hittites, Canaanites, Philistines, Edomites, etc. Dear friend, when is the last time you met a Hittite? A Philistine? They have long since passed off the scene. Yet the Jews remain! They were persecuted horribly, six million dying in Hitler's horrendous Holocaust. For 2,500 years they were without political independence, and for almost 2,000 years (from the fall of Jerusalem in A.D. 70 to 1948) they had no land of their own. They were scattered worldwide, but they were not assimilated like the Anglos, Saxons, and Jutes, or the Goths or Visigoths. Nor were they exterminated like countless others, and miraculously they retain their identity today! In Hungary, there are Hungarian Jews, and there are American Jews, Soviet Jews, English Jews, Polish Jews, etc. No other nation has ever returned to life after being so persecuted and dispossessed, but God said the Jews would! They did, another proof that the Bible is God's Word!

Men like Increase Mather saw this truth in the Bible and preached that the Jews would return to Palestine and reestablish their own nation again, and he preached it in 1669, as reported by Hal Lindsey in *The Late Great Planet Earth*. This is no "after the fact" application of some vague generalities to a historical event, but a precise fulfillment of prophecy men of God had been expecting for centuries. Suddenly, it happened! During and after World War II Jews began returning to Palestine, fleeing persecution in Germany, Europe and Russia (at one point, the Jewish population of Palestine had shrunk to about 10,000). They were joined by many affluent Jews around the world, some from America. Imagine that! Why? This inexplicable urge of many to return to a "homeland" after 2,000 years was not because they believed in the Biblical prophecy. However, the return of the Jews to Palestine fulfilled exactly what God said would happen. The British, in charge of Palestine at the time, put their gleaming warships in the way, but did not know what to do with unarmed men, women and children in merchant ships. Finally, the Jews were allowed in. Miracle of miracles, they declared themselves a nation on May 14, 1948! With heavy odds against them, they were attacked a week later by neighboring forces. They were heavily outnumbered, but they survived and conquered. They survived again when they were attacked in 1967 and in the 1970s. The Arabs had controlled Jerusalem, but now that city too is under Jewish control. (See Luke 21:24.) God's Word continues to be fulfilled and will be!

It would take far more faith to believe that this all happened by chance, than simply to believe that God gave us His Word, the Bible.

Jesus Christ - God's Living Word
"... and the Word was God." John 1:1-3, 14

The Bible claims that Jesus Christ is the Son of God. The Bible also claims that the Son Himself is God, who took upon Himself human flesh, and visited earth on a dramatic rescue mission to save men from sin, death, and Hell. Isaiah 9:6, for example, says, "For unto us a *child* is born, unto us a *son* is given, and the government shall be upon his shoulders; and his name shall be called Wonderful, Counselor, *The Mighty God, The Everlasting Father, The Prince of Peace.*" 1 Timothy 3:16 states, "And without controversy great is the mystery of godliness: *God was manifest in the flesh,* justified in the Spirit, seen of angels, preached unto the Gentiles, believed on in the world, received up to glory" (italics added). The Bible speaks of Jesus' Second Coming as "the glorious appearing of the *great God and our Saviour, Jesus Christ*" (Titus 2:13, italics added).

Jesus Himself claimed to be one with God. "He that hath seen me hath seen the Father" (John 14:9). Jesus is also called the Creator, the Resurrection and the Life, the Alpha and Omega, and possesses the names, attributes and titles of God. The apostle Thomas recognized Him as his Lord and his God (John 20:28). Jesus was worshiped as God. He performed miracles that only God could perform.

As C. S. Lewis wrote, "A man who was merely a man and said the sort of things Jesus said would not be a great moral teacher. He would either be a lunatic—on a level with the man who says he is a poached egg—or else the Devil of Hell. You must take your choice. Either this man was, and is, the Son of God: or else a madman or something worse. You can shut him up for a fool, you can spit at him and kill him as a demon, or you can fall at his feet and call him Lord and God. But let us not come with any patronizing nonsense about his being a great moral teacher. He has not left that open to us. He did not intend to."

Consider the Miracle of Jesus' Life

Never was a man born like this man. As was prophesied approximately seven hundred years before His birth, He was born in Bethlehem of a certain tribe and family of the Jews (Micah 5:2), born of a virgin (Isaiah 7:14), and born at the exact time in history that the Scriptures said He would be born (Daniel 9:25, 26). An entire nation awaited His birth, something that never happened before or since to any other person in history.

Never did another man live like Him. Christ's whole life was foretold in detail: His birth, purpose, life, method of death, ministry, and resurrection. He lived the only perfect life that anyone has ever lived. All the good characteristics of all the great men that ever lived combined, could not make one Jesus. He and He alone was absolutely flawless, without sin. He asked those who hated Him to identify one sin He had committed, but they could not.

Never did another man make such stupendous, specific claims. He claimed to be the "door" (John 10:9), and "the way, the truth, and the life" (John 14:6), the only way to heaven, to the Father. He claimed to be God in the flesh (John 8:58), forgave sins as God (Matthew 9:2-8), and accepted worship as God (e.g., Mathew 28:17).

Never did another man die as this man died. As was foretold in the Bible hundreds of years before the fact, Jesus died pierced on a cross. This was an unknown method of execution when the predictions were given (see, for example, Psalm 22:16). Over three hundred predictions were literally, precisely, and perfectly fulfilled in His birth, life, death and resurrection; and about thirty of them were realized on the very day He was crucified. Some of the predictions fulfilled on that day were that He would be pierced, wounded, and bruised, that He would be given vinegar to drink, that soldiers would gamble for His clothing, that He would die with transgressors (thieves, criminals), that He would be buried, nevertheless, in a rich man's tomb, and that not one of His bones would be broken. Incredibly, every prediction was completely fulfilled! As Dr. Peter Stoner has shown in his dynamic book *Science Speaks,* this is powerful, irrefutable evidence. Using just eight detailed prophecies about Jesus, he shows that the chance of them being fulfilled in one man by chance alone has about the same mathematical probability as covering the state of Texas two feet deep in silver dollars with just *one* of those dollars marked, and then having a blind-folded person pick out the marked dollar in just *one* try!

Never did any other man die for such a purpose as this man. As God's Word in the Old and the New Testaments makes clear, Jesus came to die for us, to take our place, to shed His blood on the cross for us. Through His tears and His pain on the cross, Jesus said,"Father, forgive them" (Luke 23:34). No one ever loved us so, and if we cannot trust Jesus, who died for us, who can we trust?

No other man ever rose from the grave, conquering death. The founders of the world's religions, Buddha, Confucius, Muhammad, are all dead, their bodies have long since decayed. Only Jesus Christ arose from the grave. Only Jesus had power over death. His tomb is empty!

Arguments Against the Resurrection

Consider briefly various arguments given by some of the world's most intelligent men who have tried to deny the resurrection.

"The disciples stole the body." In truth, however, the chief priests and elders bribed the soldiers with money to say that the disciples stole the body while the soldiers were asleep (Matt. 28:11-15). The frightened disciples had fled the horrors of the cross! Would they then defy the power of Rome for a dead body? Would all the soldiers have slept simultaneously

knowing that their very lives would be at stake if this had truly occurred? How could the disciples have moved among them and moved the huge rock that sealed the tomb without awakening the soldiers? Besides, if the soldiers had been asleep, how would they have known that the disciples stole the body?

"*The soldiers stole the body.*" Why? To risk their lives? Absurd. These tormentors and persecutors of Christians could have demolished Christianity and the disciples' claims about Christ's resurrection simply by producing the body—if they had stolen it. And, if true, why would the disciples lie about the resurrection and even risk their lives for something that never happened?

"*Jesus swooned, was put in the tomb while yet alive, revived, pushed the stone away, and came forth.*" Jesus was killed, pierced, and mutilated with a spear thrust through his side to his heart, so that the blood and water ran forth. The Roman soldiers did not even break His legs, as they did the legs of the two thieves, because He was already dead. So how could Jesus, mortally wounded, freely bleeding, and left alone for three days in a tomb, remain alive? How could He walk on nail-pierced feet, or move a huge rock with wounded hands and stagger past the soldiers without disturbing them? How could Joseph of Arimathaea, who wrapped Jesus in a clean linen cloth, not notice that He was alive? (Nicodemus and Joseph had wrapped one hundred pounds of spices around the body of Jesus in the wrapping cloth, which tended to glue and harden, so escape would have been impossible [John 19:38-42]). It takes far more faith to believe nonsense like the swoon theory, than to simply believe the truth. Jesus arose from the dead!

"*The disciples suffered from hallucinations: they wanted to see Jesus so much that they had a vision of Him.*" In that case the soldiers must have had hallucinations also. Otherwise, how can one explain the angels and the *empty tomb?* The fact remains, the *body* of Jesus Christ was gone! Besides that, imagine five hundred people having the same hallucination at the same time in broad daylight (1 Corinthians 15:6). For people prone to hallucinations, the hallucinations usually increase in intensity and frequency, but the very opposite happened when Jesus Christ ascended into heaven after appearing to His disciples. The fact is that the disciples saw the risen Christ, and went forth to tell the good news. They were freed from doubt and fear of death and rejoiced to suffer shame and even death for Jesus Christ. Nothing can account for the dramatic sudden change in their lives except the bodily resurrection of Jesus Christ!

Several other speculations attempt to explain away the resurrection, such as mistaken identity, the body dissolving into gas, and the disciples going to the wrong tomb. But these efforts are futile, foolish, and factually unfounded.

Let us carefully consider a few more facts about the resurrection. Jesus Christ was undeniably dead. The Roman centurion was an expert on death. He was made a centurion not only for his bravery in battle, but also his effectiveness in killing the enemy, and his astuteness. One of his tasks, as pointed out by a lawyer-pastor friend, Dr. Bob Topartzer, was to check on the dead after a battle to see if they were really dead, or just playing possum. In Mark 15:44, Pilate, recognizing this expertise, asked the centurion about how long Jesus had been dead. The centurion had examined Jesus. He knew He was dead. The soldiers knew Jesus was dead. They did not even break his legs. (And thus unwittingly fulfilled prophecy! Not a bone of Him was to be broken! —see Psalm 34:20) Remember, as we pointed out previously, one soldier had thrust a spear into His side, rupturing the heart sac, and blood and water had run forth. The disciples knew He was dead. They had heard Him say He would die and rise again, and the horror of His death had begun to cause them despair. The women, including Jesus' mother, knew He was dead. Later they brought spices to embalm the body. Pilate knew He was dead, as did the Jewish officials. They demanded a seal for His tomb. Joseph of Arimathaea knew He was dead, as did Nicodemus. They are the ones who took the body and wrapped it in linen with 100 pounds of spices, and put it in Joseph's tomb. Jesus was dead.

Jesus Christ was undeniably buried in the tomb of a rich man, Joseph of Arimathaea. Joseph knew Jesus was buried—it was his tomb. Nicodemus knew it. He helped Joseph of Arimathaea bury Jesus. The women knew it (Mark 15:47). They watched His burial. The soldiers knew it. Their very lives depended on the body staying in the tomb. It would be exceedingly naive to believe that they did not thoroughly check the body before they sealed the tomb. Jesus was buried.

That leaves only one real alternative. Resurrection. The bodily resurrection of the Lord Jesus Christ. The tomb was empty and it remains empty today!

Think of it! The disciples were proclaiming the resurrection of one condemned as a criminal. They proclaimed this at a time when Jerusalem was believed to be crowded with up to a million people. They grew bolder and bolder in declaring the message, especially after Pentecost. Bible scholars estimate that at least 125,000 Jews were converted to Christ in Jerusalem the first year after the resurrection! The evidence, the *empty tomb,* was right there!

The disciples knew all Jerusalem was thoroughly aware of the crucifixion of Jesus and His burial. By publicly declaring that He had conquered death and had risen from the tomb, they virtually dared any skeptic, *anyone,* friend or foe, to walk the short distance to the tomb and see for themselves! No one could deny that the body had been in the tomb. No one could say that Jesus Christ had not been dead and buried. No one, even the most bitter enemies of Christ, tried! They would have been branded as fools. Jesus had been dead. He had been buried in the tomb. Now the body was gone. The tomb was empty. Both the friends and enemies of Christ agreed on this.

Compelling Evidence ——————————————————— **17**

They had no other choice. It was an established fact. Thousands could verify it then. Millions can and have since. The tomb is still empty.

The appearances of Jesus Christ, again and again, to the disciples, to the women, to over 500 people at once, solidified the evidence.

Over 500 people watched the ascension of Jesus Christ into the clouds (compare Luke 24:33 with Luke 24:50, 51, 1 Corinthians 15:6, and Acts 1:9). This event had to have happened or it would never have been included in the scriptures. Many of the disciples, many of the 500 who were there were still alive when these scriptures were written. They would have denied the ascension of Jesus and destroyed the credibility of the Bible, had the event never occurred. They knew. They were there!

The event foreshadowed and predicted in the Old Testament hundreds of years before had come to pass. Not only the death, but the Resurrection of Jesus Christ. Among many other things, it was foretold in Isaiah 53 that Jesus would die in intense suffering for others, but in other scriptures it was plainly declared that He would reign forever. Impossible . . . without the resurrection, which is exactly what was being predicted. In Leviticus 14:1-7, God directed that a bird was to be killed in sacrifice, picturing Christ's death on the cross, and the blood of that bird was to be sprinkled on a living bird which then was to be set free! The living bird symbolized Christ's resurrection! This was a picture of the death and resurrection of Jesus Christ! Then Jesus Himself told His disciples that He would die and rise again the third day. He did.

Another tremendous testimony to the resurrection of Jesus Christ is found in Leviticus 23:9-11 as explained in 1 Corinthians 15:20. In Leviticus God instructs the children of Israel to remember that when they begin to reap the harvest, they are to bring a sheaf of the *firstfruits* of the harvest to the priest. The priest was to wave the sheaf of firstfruits *"on the morrow," after the sabbath,* to be accepted as an offering for them. 1 Corinthians 15:20 informs us that the firstfruits is *Christ.* The Jewish *sabbath* was *Saturday!* The "morrow after the sabbath" is *Sunday!* It was God's way of introducing a new day honoring the resurrected Christ! God had given very specific instructions to the Jews concerning keeping the Sabbath. It was part of the covenant with God, of the whole Sabbath structure involving letting the land lay idle one year out of seven. This included the Jubilee year, measured by seven times seven, or 49 Sabbatical years. Debts were rescinded, houses and possessions returned, servants set free in this glorious fiftieth year. The loss of any part of the structure decimated the whole. The Sabbath was given particularly to the Jews. Death could be the penalty for breaking it, or not observing it. The fact that converted Jews *risked their lives* by celebrating Sunday in place of Saturday is a strong witness to the resurrection of Christ!

Special celebration days have historical significance. We celebrate July 4 in honor of the signing of the Declaration of Independence. July 4 celebrates a historical fact. So it is with other special days. As Josh McDowell correctly points out, "Sunday is the only day that celebrates a historical fact 52 days a year!" That fact is the resurrection of Jesus Christ!

As we have said, one of the powerful testimonies to the fact of the resurrection of Christ is that thousands of Jews, at the risk of all they owned, even of their lives, began to worship God on a new day, Sunday! Jews were the first converts. Imagine the courage and conviction it took for them to step out and change their day. This was done in spite of centuries of Sabbath keeping, in spite of families and loved ones, in spite of certain loss. Nothing can account for this change but the resurrection of Jesus Christ.

All of this brings us to the indisputable fact that the disciples were transformed from mice to martyrs by the resurrection of Jesus Christ. Does it make sense that they suffer the loss of homes, families, and careers for a lie? Why would they suffer loneliness, hunger, cold, and torture and death, for a lie? Why would they even rejoice in their losses, and die rejoicing? They had *everything* to lose, and *nothing* to gain, unless the resurrection of Jesus Christ was a *fact!* Nearly all, if not all, of the disciples of Jesus Christ died a martyr's death. They knew the truth about His death and resurrection. Since then, it is estimated that some 66 million Christians have been martyred for Christ.

The *fact* is the disciples saw the risen Christ, and flamed forth to tell the good news. They were freed from doubt and fear of death and rejoiced to suffer shame and even death for Jesus Christ. *Nothing can account for the dramatic, sudden change in their lives except the bodily resurrection of Jesus Christ! They saw Him. Jesus conquered death. His claims are true!*

The Miracle of Changed Lives

"No man can change lives like Jesus Christ. "Therefore if any man be in Christ, he is a new creature: old things are passed away; behold, all things are become new" (2 Corinthians 5:17).

Saul, the religious bigot and murderer, became Paul, the mighty missionary for Jesus Christ as a result of an encounter on the Damascus road with the risen Christ. This same life-changing conversion has happened to millions since who have put their trust in Him. I have never met a prostitute, or an alcoholic, or a drug addict who has said to me, "I met George Washington, or Abraham Lincoln, the other day, and he changed my life!" But I have met many in these categories who have said, "I met Jesus Christ the other day, and He changed my life!" Why? Because He is alive!

One night in Anchorage I counseled Ed Perry. Ed was a very heavy drinker, a rough, ungodly man. A professing agnostic, he was embittered by a physical tragedy in the family. He was also a former semipro football player. When I finally got an opportunity to talk alone with him he firmly resisted the Gospel.

To Ed's and my surprise, I abruptly interrupted our verbal sparring and said, "Ed Perry, you are going to be saved in five minutes." I marched over to his side, opened the Bible, and showed Ed how to become a Christian. Ed was saved, his bitterness gone forever, and his whole pattern of life radically changed. If you find this story hard to believe, ask the Rev. Ed Perry, now a pastor in Everett, Washington. Ed could add many other things to this story. His life was sick with sin and shame until Jesus delivered him. What else or who else can change a man like that but Christ!

Consider another miracle: Josh McDowell was a brilliant young man. However, he had a very sad childhood and was an unhappy young man. His father was a town drunk. His friends laughed at his father's drunken escapades. When Josh's friends came over, he would even take his father out to the barn and tie him up. Then he would park the car near the silo and tell his friends his father was not home! While laughing on the outside, Josh cringed on the inside. In a small town, few things are worse than having your father be the town alcoholic.

Josh was generally an angry young man, but he especially hated his father. On one occasion he had seen his mother lying in the manure behind the cows in the barn. Josh's father had beaten her so badly that she could not even stand up. One can only imagine the rage and hate that filled Josh's heart.

Slowly the years passed. Josh went off to college and met some genuine born-again Christians. He saw in them something for which his hungry heart longed, yet his intellect was not ready to accept. So Josh purposed to "intellectually refute" Christianity and the resurrection of Jesus Christ. He dug determinedly into the evidence. The battle for his mind and heart was monumental. Finally, convinced but still reluctant,

Josh did what he felt was the only honest thing he could do. While alone in his room, he invited Jesus Christ into the his heart and life on December 19, 1959 at 8:30 p.m. It was a quiet unemotional conversion, based on evidence and the reality of the risen Christ. But what began as a relatively uneventful conversion, later became an explosive transformation. Josh tells of debating the head of the history department at a midwestern university when the professor challenged him to name some concrete changes Christ had made in his life. Forty-five minutes later the professor asked him to stop!

Some of the changes that Jesus Christ has made in Josh McDowell's life include taking away his fierce temper and giving deep peace to his restless mind, and replacing his insecurity with assurance. God also gave Josh a passion to reach other people for Jesus Christ.

Josh experienced another astonishing change after he had accepted Christ. Slowly but surely God began to replace the burning hatred in his heart for his father. About five months after receiving Christ, the love of Christ so overpowered Josh that he looked his father in the eye and told him, "Dad, I love you!"

Sometime later when Josh was at home his father came into his room and asked Josh how he could possibly love a father like him? Josh told his dad that just six months earlier he had despised him! Then Josh told him how Jesus Christ had come into his life. He told his dad that Jesus had turned his hate into love, and that now he truly loved his dad. Forty-five minutes later, Josh experienced one of the greatest thrills of his life. His father, who had known Josh and his hatred, simply said, "Son, if God can do in my life what I've seen Him do in yours, then I want to give Him the opportunity." Then and there a miracle occurred. Josh's alcoholic dad prayed with him, and trusted Christ as his Lord and Savior. The life of Josh's father changed from night to day. No longer was he an alcoholic. He was truly a new creature in Christ.

Since then Josh McDowell has become internationally famous. Some of his books such as *Evidence That Demands a Verdict* and *More Evidence That Demands a Verdict* are classics and contain a mass of historical evidence of the Christian faith and Scriptures. Josh has spoken in more than six hundred universities. He has debated skeptics, atheists, and unbelieving religious leaders all over the world.

Herbert VanderLugt shares another thrilling story of the transformation Christ can make in a person's life:

> I had no idea what my grandson meant when he told me he wanted a Transformer. Then he explained that it is a toy that can be changed from robot to tank to truck and back to robot again. Seeing one helped me understand how it got its name. But it also made me think about life's ultimate transformation—the one that Jesus Christ produces in the lives of all who trust Him.
>
> Oscar Cervantes is a dramatic example of Christ's power to transform lives. As a child, Oscar began to get into trouble. Then as he got older, he was jailed 17 times for brutal crimes. Prison psychiatrists said he was beyond help. But they were wrong! During a brief interval of freedom, Oscar met an elderly man who told him about Jesus. He placed his trust in the Lord and was changed into a kind, caring man. Shortly afterward he started a prison ministry. Chaplain H.C. Warwick describes it this way: "The third Saturday night of each month is 'Oscar Night' at Soledad. Inmates come to hear Oscar and they sing gospel songs with fervor; they sit intently for over 2 hours; they come freely to the chapel altar... What professionals had failed to do for Oscar in years of counseling, Christ did in a moment of conversion."
>
> In Mark 5 we read that Jesus Christ turned a raging, demon-possessed maniac into a docile, normal man. The same power that changed the maniac and Oscar Cervantes is available to all who trust Jesus. He is the Master Transformer. Has He changed you?

As Josh McDowell has pointed out in his dynamic book, *More Than a Carpenter,* Jesus Christ had to have been either a liar, a lunatic, or the Lord God. It is impossible that Jesus Christ was a liar. He was the epitome of honesty, and demanded that people be honest at any cost. Everything He said came true. He gave His own life for what He said was true.

He was no lunatic. Rather He was the essence of sanity and tranquility under intense pressure, false accusations, persecution, and death. His impeccable character and serene demeanor negate this possibility.

The only other viable alternative? Jesus Christ was and is the Lord God! Tens of millions have testified that Christ has changed their lives, answered their deepest needs, satisfied their longings, and given them peace. These transformed individuals include former White House special counsel Chuck Colson, scientists Dr. Henry Morris and Dr. Duane Gish, pro football players Steve Largent and Roosevelt Grier, former Dallas Cowboy head coach Tom Landry, ice skater Janet Lynn, pro basketball player "Dr. J." Julius Erving, scholar Josh McDowell, some sixty-six million martyrs who have been tortured and slain for Jesus, and millions of other "ordinary" people. From them and others the cry of praise goes up, "Jesus died for me, and I love Him, and He is alive. He loves me, He has saved me, He dwells in me, and He has changed my life!"

Has He changed your life?

D. L. Moody was a powerful evangelist for the Lord Jesus Christ. God used him to rock two continents for Christ. Once he was asked if he had "dying grace." Moody replied that he did not. He said in effect that he had living grace. But he added that when the time came to die, he would have dying grace. Indeed he did.

Many years later, as Moody began to die he said triumphantly, "Heaven is opening . . . earth is receding . . . Jesus is coming."

Beloved friend, which way do you want to die? With Jesus Christ, life can be beautiful, and death ushers in a glorious new world for you. What does death hold for you?

We have appealed both to your heart and mind. We can do no more. We cannot possibly verbalize the glory and wonder of Jesus Christ, but if the Holy Spirit of God takes this stumbling effort and reveals the reality of Christ to you so that you *want* Him, we will be happy beyond words. Only God's Spirit *can* reveal Christ to you, and then only if you are *willing* to see. Jesus warns, *now* is the day of salvation. *Today*, if you hear His voice, harden not your heart (2 Corinthians 6:2).

Perhaps, as you read you felt either vaguely or acutely uncomfortable. You may have felt "pressured." Beloved, it is hard to do a "soft sell" to awaken your wife and child when you know the house is on fire. Paul Revere had little time for social chitchat on his wild night ride, however less offensive it might have been. The message was urgent, and far more so is the message of the Cross.

When I was in the Navy and suicide planes were attacking us off Okinawa, I noticed a peculiar reaction, much like that of Pavlov's dog. We had a buzzer which signaled the alert for action time and time again. After awhile, we sailors experienced knots in the pit of our stomachs, dry mouths, and intense reactions when the buzzer sounded, usually long before planes were sighted. We began to actually resent the *buzzer!* Yet had we put ear plugs in our ears, or ignored the buzzer we would have been killed. Many times our instant response to the buzzer got us in position to defend our ship and our lives before the enemy came. The buzzer was our best friend and actually startled us into saving our lives.

The gospel shocks one out of his mental or moral apathy. One can then either apply ear plugs, ignore the alarm of conviction, the nagging uneasiness, or quickly respond and honestly confront and accept the risen Christ, who secures us against all enemies. Sometimes there is but one alarm, and it may be but faintly heard amidst the strident clamor of the world. Please don't ignore the alarm.

No one ever *cared* for you—like Jesus! Religion won't do. I've led Bible teachers, Bible School graduates, even missionaries, to Christ or to assurance of their salvation. Only knowing Him will ever really satisfy and suffice.

In a way, it's much like the little boy who said to the atheist who was deriding him because he was so happy that his alcoholic Dad had accepted Christ. The atheist chided the boy for being so naive as to believe the myth of the Bible and that old-fashioned stuff about being "saved." He closed his statement by exclaiming, "Boy, you're dreaming!" The boy replied aptly, "Mister, Dad used to come home and beat and kick me. I'd hide in terror when I heard him come staggering home. He cursed and beat my dear Mom and we were often cold and hungry and short of clothes, and Mother cried a lot. Now Dad buys nice clothes for Mother, and kisses and hugs her. He takes me on his lap and tells me stories and tells me he loves me. Our home is warm and snug and we all love Jesus. Mister, if I'm dreaming, please don't wake me up!"

Friend, Jesus frees us from enemies more subtle and deadly than alcohol, doubt, insecurity, hopelessness, dread, fear, anguish, purposelessness, uncertainty. He frees us from sin and Hell. Through Him you can know and experience abundant life.

In writing this book I have one desire—to point you to Jesus now! It was His heartbeat you felt, my friend, and from the bloody cross, the empty tomb, and now at your heart's door He pleads with you. Eternity—one heartbeat away—so long, so endless. "Let me into your heart and life. I, Jesus Christ love you!"

Just in case it is still not clear exactly how to be saved, how to accept Jesus, to believe savingly on Him, and know for sure that you have been saved, please read the next chapter, *Salvation: Clear and Biblical.*

One Solitary Life

Nearly two thousand years ago in an obscure village, a child was born of a peasant woman. He grew up in another village where He worked as a carpenter until He was thirty. Then for three years He became an itinerant preacher.

This Man never went to college or seminary. He never wrote a book. He never held a public office. He never had a family or owned a home. He never put His foot inside a big city nor traveled even two hundred miles from His birthplace. And though He never did any of the things that usually accompany greatness, throngs of people followed Him. He had no credentials but Himself.

While He was still young, the tide of public opinion turned against Him. His followers ran away. He was turned over to His enemies and went through the mockery of a trial. He was sentenced to die on a cross between two thieves. While he was dying, His executioners gambled for the only piece of property He had on earth—the simple coat He had worn. His body was laid in a borrowed grave provided by a compassionate friend.

But three days later this Man arose from the dead—living proof that He was, as He had claimed, the Savior whom God had sent, the incarnate Son of God.

Nearly twenty centuries have come and gone and today the risen Lord Jesus Christ is the central figure of the human race. On our calendars His birth divides history into two eras. One day of every week is set aside in remembrance of Him. And our two most important holidays celebrate His birth and resurrection. On church steeples around the world His cross has become the symbol of victory over sin and death.

This one Man's life has furnished the theme for more songs, books, poems, and paintings than any other person or event in history. Thousands of colleges, hospitals, orphanages, and other institutions have been founded in honor of this One who gave His life for us.

All the armies that ever marched, all the navies that ever sailed, all the governments that ever sat, all the kings that ever reigned have not changed the course of history as much as this *one* solitary life.

Over the centuries millions have found a new life of forgiveness from sins and peace with God through faith in Jesus Christ. Today He offers this life to all who will believe. "I am the way, the truth, and the life," Jesus said, "no man cometh unto the Father, but by me." "He that heareth my word, and believeth on him that sent me, hath everlasting life, and shall not come into condemnation, but is passed from death unto life" (John 14:6; 5:24).

Has the Lord Jesus Christ changed your life?

Ask Him . . . Trust Him . . . He Will!

Weighing the Evidence

We have briefly stated some of the compelling evidence for the Bible and for Jesus Christ. Can we identify Jesus Christ beyond a shadow of a doubt as being who He claimed to be? Please consider the evidence one more time. God will not force you to believe. You must make that final choice. But to fail to act on that evidence will haunt you for a billion years in Hell, and that breaks my heart for you.

When I was a sailor, I had several "blind dates." Suppose for this particular blind date, I agree to meet her at the Greyhound Bus Station, 464 Liberty Street, tonight at 8:00 p.m. She tells me she is one-legged, and wears a peg-leg on her left leg which she has painted florescent yellow with a blinking red light built in it to keep folks from stumbling over it. She also has a matching florescent yellow patch over her right eye which she lost in the same accident in which she lost her leg. Also, she is missing the little finger on her right hand. She will wear a pink stocking on her good leg and a maroon and white saddle oxford on her one good foot. She will wear a green hat and a lavender dress and will carry a purple purse. She says she is five feet tall and weighs about 200 hundred pounds. Do you honestly think I would have any trouble identifying the right girl at the Greyhound Bus Station at 8:00 p.m.?

Remember, the *time* of Jesus Christ's birth was foretold centuries in advance (Daniel 9:24-26). This does away with the otherwise possible objection that is sometimes made that one could make *any* prophecy and something would eventually occur which could be labeled as the fulfillment of that prophecy. The time element destroys this objection.

I gave only 13 or 14 identification marks concerning my blind date. However, the chances are millions to one against there being another girl with these same identifying characteristics in that particular bus station at 8:00 p.m.! God gave 333 marks of identification for Jesus, concerning His birth, death and resurrection. Each mark of identification was fulfilled perfectly in Jesus, so there could be no doubt about identifying Him when He came, and verifying His identity now that He has come! Remember, everything Christ said came true. He said Hell was real and forever, just as Heaven is. A million years from now you will be somewhere. Will it be in Heaven or in Hell?

Every prophecy of the Bible is always accurately, literally fulfilled. To get the full impact of this, suppose some prognosticator predicted 100 things that would happen to you in the coming year. Many of these predictions are very detailed. The first prediction is that you will stub your toe on a chair leg on January first at 12:35 a.m., just past midnight. You will fall on a glass on the kitchen table, which will shatter and cut a U-shaped wound in your chin. This jagged wound will require 13 stitches. It will be sewn up by a new doctor in town named McGuire, your doctor being unavailable at the time. To your chagrin and amazement, when January first comes, this is *exactly* what happens, right down to the smallest detail!

Then, throughout the year, 99 of these prophecies are literally, actually, perfectly fulfilled in every detail. Ninety-nine of the 100, with one more to go! This last prophecy is for the last day of the year. It declares that if you drive downtown to Fifth and Main at 5:00 p.m. you will be in a fiery car crash that will leave you blind and crippled and badly burned. You will be in excruciating pain. You will be hospitalized for six months and then die.

Tell me, would you deliberately drive down to Fifth and Main at 5:00 p.m. on the last day of the year if you had a choice? Would you consider it a safe, sane, intelligent risk when 99 prophecies have come true without a failure, which would be virtually impossible mathematically by chance alone?

Let's round the Bible prophecies off to 100, 99 of which have already been perfectly fulfilled. The one-hundredth prophecy is that if you ignore or refuse to accept Jesus Christ as your personal Lord and Savior, you will die without hope and spend eternity in the Lake of Fire spoken of in Revelation chapter 20 as the destiny of the lost. A billion years from now your agony and depair and lostness from His love will have barely begun. Since all the other Bible prophecies have come true in literal and absolute fact, would it be intelligent to gamble your destiny forever that this last and final prophecy will not also come true?

Beloved friend, it is so good to have Jesus and His abundant life and peace even now, in this life, as well as settling your eternal destiny forever to be sure of being in Heaven with Him! How unutterably sweet it is to have your sins forgiven, to be saved and know it, to lay your head on your pillow at night absolutely sure that you will be in Heaven with Jesus forever.

Jesus loves you so much. He proved it on the bloody cross when He died for you and me in our place. Read the next chapter very carefully in order to know how to be saved forever and sure of it. Do it *now!* Nothing in this world is so urgent, or so important. Turn now to chapter two, *"Salvation: Clear and Biblical."*

2

Salvation: Clear and Biblical

Step One: *God loves you and wants you to know that there is only One God.* This *one God* created the universe and is *Lord* over all. "In the beginning God created the heaven and the earth" (Genesis 1:1).

". . . before me there was no God formed, neither shall there be after me" (Isaiah 43:10b).

God was *never* a man, and man will *never* be God! As the eternal God he became the *God-man* Jesus, to die for us, but for all eternity he was God, not man.

". . . from everlasting (that's *eternity past)* to everlasting (that's *eternity future) Thou art God!* (Psalm 90:2b).

God never progressed, earned or attained His way to being God, *He was always God.* (The Bible mentions false gods, but to believe that other gods really exist is pagan polytheism, not Christianity.)

Clearly, there is not now, and never will be, any other God on this planet or any other "world" or planet. There is forever only *one* God. Men cannot become Gods—none ever has, none ever will!

". . . for I am God, and there is none else; I am God, and there is none like me" (Isaiah 46:9b). ". . . before me there was no

God formed, neither shall there be after me" (Isaiah 43:10b).

Step Two: *There is One Saviour, Jesus Christ, Who is Eternally God.*

"For unto us a child is born, unto us a son is given: and the government shall be upon His shoulders, and His name shall be called Wonderful, Counsellor, The mighty God, The everlasting Father, the Prince of Peace" (Isaiah 9:6). Within the nature of God there are three eternal distinctions or Persons: God the Father, God the Son, and God the Holy Spirit; there is only *one God*. Since Jesus is repeatedly called God, we must accept Him as God, or we accept another Jesus. In the Bible the "Word" means Jesus (John 1:14). "In the beginning was the Word, and the Word was with God, and the Word was God" (John 1:1). "Beginning" here simply means, *"from all time."* As God was God *from all time* so was Jesus Christ God, from the beginning, *from all time!* Jesus never progressed, worked, or attained His way into being God, *He was always God* (Micah 5:2).

God forbade forever the worship of any other god (Exod. 34:14), yet Jesus accepted worship as God on many occasions. "And as they went to tell his disciples, behold, Jesus met them saying, All hail. And they came and held Him by the feet and worshipped Him" (Matthew 28:9). No wonder Thomas cried out to Jesus, "My Lord and my God" (John 20:28).

Step Three: *The Sin Problem—Our Sin Nature*

An apple tree is an apple tree *before* it bears apples. It bears apples *because* it is an apple tree.

So, we sin *because* we have a sin nature. We are all by "nature the children of wrath" (Ephesians 2:3). An apple tree is just as much an apple tree by nature, whether it bears one apple or a thousand! So it is with a sinner.

One sin or a thousand is not the point! The point is, we *all* have a sin nature that must be changed.

> Just as picking the fruit off an apple tree does not change the nature of the tree (it's still an apple tree!), so getting rid of some sins in our lives does not change our sin nature!

Picking the apples off the tree does not change the nature of the tree! So, getting rid of some sins does not change our nature!

"Ye must be born again" (John 3:7). John 1:12 tells us how: "But as many as received Him, to them gave He power to become the sons of God, even to them that believe on His name."

We are *not* by nature children of God. We must receive Christ in order to *become* the children of God.

We are sinners by nature and choice. Sin is the fruit of our sin nature, of each of us as sinners. Sin is "going our own way" (Isaiah 53:6). It is being the God, Manager, Boss, Lord of our own life. It is being self-centered instead of Christ-centered.

"For by grace are ye saved through faith; and that not of yourselves: it is the gift of God: Not of works, lest any man should boast" (Ephesians 2:8, 9). "There is none righteous, no, not one" (Romans 3:10b).

"Now to him that worketh (for salvation) is the reward not reckoned of grace, but of debt. But to him that worketh not, but believeth on Him that justifieth the ungodly, his faith is counted for righteousness" (Romans 4:4-6).

Salvation is not by works, it is a *gift*. Personally receiving Christ, trusting Him alone to save us, is God's way of salvation. "For the wages of sin is death, but the gift of God is eternal life through Jesus Christ, our Lord" (Rom. 6:23).

We cannot make ourselves "worthy" of the grace of God. Salvation is a free gift for the unworthy, the undeserving, which we all are. Christ died for the "ungodly" (Rom. 5:6).

A dog does not bark in order to become a dog. He barks because he already is a dog. His barking helps demonstrate

"NOT BY WORKS"

BAPTISM
CHURCH TITHES
GOOD WORKS

"For by grace are ye saved through faith; and that not of yourselves: it is the gift of God: *Not of works...* " Eph. 2:8,9

How many *good works* can a *dead* man do? As natural men we are *all,* " dead in trespasses and sins." Ephesians 2:1b

the fact! Just so, we do not do good works in order to become Christians (be saved). We do good works *after* we are saved (become Christians) to demonstrate the fact that we have been saved.

Remember that God's Word says, *before* salvation, "All our righteousness are as filthy rags" (Isaiah 64:6b). We all have a sinful nature. We are sinners by nature and by choice. "For all have sinned and come short of the glory of God" (Romans 3:23). This means we are all *lost* sinners. Besides, how many *good works* can a *dead* man do? As natural men we are all "dead in trespasses and sins" (Ephesians 2:1b).

Although salvation is not by works, true salvation always produces a changed life. Christ comes in by personal invitation as Lord and Savior to change our life, and live His life through us.

The Good News is . . . the blood of Jesus Christ, God's Son, cleanses us from all sin (1 John 1:9).

Salvation: Clear and Biblical

> "The Blood of Jesus Christ, God's Son, cleanses us from all sin."
> 1 John 1:9

Step Four: *The Time is Now.*

After death it is too late. Now is the time to be saved. ". . . now is the accepted time; behold, now is the day of salvation" (2 Corinthians 6:2b). There is no chance after death. "And as it is appointed unto men once to die, but after this the judgment" (Hebrews 9:27). There is no general salvation for all men because of Christ's death, but only individual salvation for those who believe. ". . . he that believeth not the Son shall not see life; but the wrath of God abideth on him" (John 3:36b). All men are resurrected, but the unsaved dead are resurrected to damnation, not salvation (John 5:29; Revelation 19:3-6).

"And whosoever was not found written in the book of life was cast into the lake of fire" (Revelation 20:15). Nowhere in the Bible is anyone ever said to have been saved after they died. Today is the day of salvation.

"Enter ye in at the strait gate: for wide is the gate, and broad is the way, that leadeth to destruction, and many there be which go in thereat. Because strait is the gate, and narrow is the way, which leadeth unto life, and few there be that find it" (Matthew 7:13, 14).

According to God's Word, the vast multitude of men are on the road to Hell, and to the resurrection unto damnation (John 5:29) unless they personally invite Christ into their lives as Lord and Savior. Death ends all hope for the lost.

Because of our sin nature all men are sinners, both by what we are and what we do. That is why Jesus said, "Ye must be born again" (John 3:7).

Suppose a pig tried to become a sheep by *acting* like a sheep. Suppose the pig was clothed in sheep wool, ate sheep feed and even learned to bleat like a sheep. Would that *change* its pig nature and make it a sheep?

Would it matter whether or not the pig was "good" or "bad" by pig standards? So it is with trying to *act* like a Christian in order to become a Christian! It takes a miracle—the new birth. Just as it would take a miracle from God, a new birth, for a pig to become a sheep, so it takes a miracle from God, the new birth, for a sinner to become a child of God, a Christian.

"But as many as received Him, to them gave He power to become the sons of God, even to them that believe on His name" (John 1:12).

Step Five: *The Way of Salvation.*
Jesus alone can cleanse us from sin and change our nature. "Who His own self bare our sins in His own body on the tree" (1 Peter 2:24). Not just Adam's sin, but our own personal sins. This is why He died on the cross for us, why He shed His blood for us, to pay the debt for our sins.

We need cleansing from sin and a new nature in order to become a Christian. Jesus took our place and shed His blood to cleanse us from sin. No amount of "good works" could wash away one sin or change our nature. "Just as I am without one plea, but that thy blood was shed for me."

Good News! Salvation is instantaneous! The moment we repent, turn to Jesus from our sins, He saves us. Christ said to the unbaptized, unsaved, no good works, thief on the cross, in instant salvation response to the thief's believing call: "Today shalt thou be with me in paradise" (Luke 23:43b). (The place Paul saw as the Heaven of God, 1 Corinthians 12:2-4). *Instant* salvation for a harlot: "Go thy way, thy faith hath saved thee" (Luke 7:50b). *Instant* salvation in response to the publican's believing call: ". . . this man went down to his house justified" (Luke 18:14a).

Saul the murderer was changed to Paul the Apostle by one vital encounter with the living Christ. Salvation includes accepting Jesus Christ as both Lord (*our* God, Lord, new manager) and Savior. It involves heart (in the Bible, 'heart' means the ruling, governing, choosing, center of our being) belief. "That if thou shalt confess with thy mouth the Lord Jesus, and shalt believe in thine heart that God hath raised him from the dead, thou shalt be saved" (Romans 10:9).

We thus turn from our sins, our self, and our way to God's way. When we believingly call on the Lord Jesus, in faith and repentance, He enters our life, cleanses us from sin, makes us children of God by the new birth, and gives us the free gift of salvation, with new, abundant, everlasting life. Heaven becomes our certain home, and His peace our possession.

There is no magic in the few puffs of air emitted from our vocal cords as we call on Christ. Yet He said, "Out of the abundance of the heart the mouth speaketh" (Matthew 12:24). If our call is from the heart, using our God-given power of choice to believe in Christ, *God always responds* and *saves! He promised!*

Salvation is simple. "For *whosoever* shall *call* upon the name of the Lord *shall be saved*" (Romans 10:13). We must personally *call believingly* on Jesus to save us. This is *how* we receive Him. If we do so call, He must save us or God would be lying, and God *cannot* lie. If Jesus loved us enough to die in bloody agony to save us, would He then turn us down when we called on Him? *Of course not!*

Remember! "God commendeth His love toward us, in that, while we were yet sinners, Christ died for us" (Romans 5:8). God *loves* us, and wants us to come to Christ just as we are. God loves *you* and wants *you* to be saved. Would you like to receive Jesus as your Lord and Saviour right now? Just pray, *if you mean it*, the best you know how, with all your heart, this prayer, or a similar one.

> "Lord Jesus Christ, come into my heart and life. Cleanse me from all sin by your shed blood. Make me a child of God. Give me your free gift of everlasting life, and let me know that I am saved, now and forever. I now receive you as my very own personal Lord and Savior. I place my complete trust in you alone for my salvation. In Jesus' name, Amen."

Did Jesus save you or did He lie? According to Romans 10:13 he had to do one or the other if you called believingly on Him. "For whosoever shall call upon the name of the Lord, shall be saved."

Salvation is certain! You can *know* you are saved, not just by *feeling*, but because God's Word says so! Memorize John 3:36a. Read it three times. "He that believeth on the Son hath

Salvation: Clear and Biblical 39

everlasting life." What do you have right now according to God's Word? Where would you go if you were to die right now, according to God's Word?

If you *know* that Jesus has saved you, according to His Word, please thank Him out loud for saving you.

"These things have I written unto you that believe on the name of the Son of God, that ye may *know* that ye have eternal life" (1 John 5:13a).

As a help to you, to further nail down this definite decision, you may wish to sign your name to the following statement:

I have today received Jesus Christ as my Lord and Savior. I am claiming by faith His promise of sins forgiven and His gift of eternal life.

Signed: _____

Date: _____

Choose to believe Christ, feelings or no feelings, and He will prove His reality to you as you step out in faith that He has kept His word and saved you.

Note this important illustration. Three men step aboard an elevator bound for the third floor where they all want to go. One is laughing, one is crying, one is poker-faced, unemotional. All three of them get to the third floor, regardless of their feelings, because they *believed* the elevator would get them to the third floor, *acted* on their belief, and *com-*

mitted themselves to the elevator. So it is with trusting Christ, feelings or no feelings.

The reality of your salvation will be shown in your love-response in obeying and following Jesus Christ "...If a man love me, he *will* (not if, maybe and/or but) keep my words" (John 14:23a). To work *for* salvation shows unbelief in the sufficiency of Jesus Christ alone to save us. However, true salvation, true faith, always produces good works! "But wilt thou know, O vain man, that faith without works is dead?" (James 2:20).

An apple tree does not have to produce apples in order to become an apple tree! Apples are products of the tree and prove that it is an apple tree. So, good works never *produce* a Christian, they merely *prove* he is one. "Therefore, if any man is in Christ, he is a new creation, old things are passed away; behold, all things are become new" (2 Corinthians 5:17).

We must have salvation in order to demonstrate it, just as we must have a car before we can demonstrate it! True Christians produce good works.

Believe Him for His victory, thank Him, step out in faith, and He will prove His victory in your experience.

In the next and final chapter some guidelines and helps for new believers are introduced and explained.

3

The Christ Changed Life

"Jesus answered and said unto him, If a man love me, he will keep my word: and my Father will love him, and we will come unto him, and make our abode with him" (John 14:23).

This list with Bible verses for you to study is given for a quick reference. A discussion of each of the eight items listed is given in this important chapter.

1. *Be baptized.* Acts 2:41, 10:47-48; 16:31-33.
2. *Confess Christ before men.* Luke 12:8-9; Romans 10:9-10.
3. *Attend church faithfully.* Hebrews 10:25; 1 John 3:14.
4. *Read the Bible daily.* Study it, and memorize special verses. Joshua 1:8; Psalm 1:2; 119:1; Colossians 3:16-17; 2 Timothy 2:15; 1 Peter 2:2. Start in the New Testament with John, then 1 John, and then go to Matthew. Read straight through the entire New Testament, then read the Old Testament.
5. *Pray daily . . . and more often.* Jeremiah 33:3; Matthew 18:19; 21:22; Romans 8:32; 1 Thessalonians 5:17;

1 John 5:14-15.
6. *Confess sin instantly, honestly, and avoid it.* Proverbs 28:13; 1 John 1:9.
7. *Share Christ . . . Witness . . . Win the lost.*
Psalms 126:6; Proverbs 11:30; Luke 5:10; 19:10; John 20:21; Acts 1:8.
8. *Let Jesus live His life through you.* 1 Cor.inthians 15:57; Gal. 2:20; 5:16; Col. 3:1-4. Live by faith, not feeling.

Faith is the *root,* feeling is the *fruit.*

About Your Decision

A definite decision for Christ is necessary and important. Life or death, Heaven or Hell, hinge upon this decision. That is why we stress the need of crystallizing belief into a concrete act of accepting Christ. We are told in the Bible to call, to receive, to be born again, to open the door.

Agrippa believed the prophets, Paul said, but was not a Christian; he did not personally receive the risen Christ. The devils believe and tremble, God says, but they are doomed to Hell forever. Obviously then, there is a belief which falls short of saving faith in Christ, short of the act of receiving Him as Savior and Lord, unconditionally.

A young man can love a young woman and she can return that love; yet they can remain apart in deepest frustration and sorrow until death. They do not belong to each other until in the simple act of marriage each consents to receive the other and forsake all others. So it is with Christ. One may profess to believe in Him, to love Him, and yet never receive Him, call on Him, open the door to Him for salvation. Saving faith then requires the act of calling on and receiving Christ and being born into the family of God. Then we are new creatures with new desires, new power, and new life (2 Corinthians 5:17).

Regardless then of how much we convince ourselves we love Him and believe in Him, we must call on Him, receive Him, open the door to Him, invite Him in by a definite decision or act of faith as the Bible says. "For whosoever shall call upon the name of the Lord shall be saved" (Romans 10:13). We trust you have made this definite decision!

If you *did ask* Jesus believingly to save you, *Welcome to God's* family! Congratulations! You have just become a child of God! You have just been born again, born from above, born of the Spirit of God into the forever family of God! You are a new creation in Christ. Your sins are washed away by His shed blood. You have a new future, a new family, and a new Father! We have just shown you from God's Word how you can be saved and know it for sure from Romans 10:13. Check also John 3:36 and 1 John 5:13 (we suggest you memorize these verses). You can rejoice with all your heart that Jesus is yours and you are His forever, that Heaven and not Hell is your eternal home, and that He will be with you in a new and vital way now and forever. Salvation is instant, the results last forever! God says you are now a "new creature in Christ." How delightful! How exciting! (2 Corinthians 5:17)

Now let me share with you how to begin and continue with your new life of love-response, obedience and growth in Christ. As a real child of God, I know you will be ready to obey the Lord Jesus Christ, just as God's Word says you will in John 14:23. Jesus answered and said unto him, If a man love me, he will keep my words: and my Father will love him, and we will come unto him, and make our abode with him."

1. Be Baptized

The waters of baptism cannot wash away one sin. That was done the moment you were saved by the shed blood of the Lord Jesus Christ. But God commanded that we be baptized as soon as we have been saved. Just as the approximately 3,000 converts in Acts 2:41 were baptized the day they were saved, and the jailer in Philippi was baptized the very night he believed and was saved (Acts 16:31-33), so we should be baptized as soon as possible after we are saved. Baptism is an outward picture of an inward cleansing. It comes after salvation; before salvation it has no value or meaning. It pictures on the outside what Christ has already done on the inside. Even more important, biblically, it pictures our death with Jesus to the old life, identifies us with His death for us, identifies us with His burial for us as we go down under the water of baptism, and identifies us with His risen life as we rise from the water of baptism as He bodily arose from the grave. We are thus publicly forever declaring our identification with the Lord Jesus Christ, our death to the old life, and declaring our new life in Him. Acts 10:47 clearly shows the order: salvation, then baptism (see also Romans 6:1-4).

Baptism fulfills the picture of death, burial, and resurrection which the Bible presents as a picture of our identification with Christ.

Stated another way, when we have been saved, God counts it that we died with Christ in His death, were buried with Him, and rose with Him to new life. Baptism pictures this! Beautiful! Do it, *not in order to be saved,* but because you have *already* been saved, and now want to fully love and obey Him!

2. Confess Christ Before Men

"Also I say unto you, Whosoever shall confess me before men, him shall the Son of man also confess before the angels of God: But he that denieth me before men shall be denied before the angels of God" (Luke 12:8, 9).

Open, public confession of Jesus Christ is Biblical evidence and confirmation of salvation. That is why many of our churches give public invitations so that before a friendly, loving crowd praying for just such miracles, you may acknowledge Christ. *God* commanded confession before men. If those early disciples in Jerusalem had declared that salvation was a private thing between them and God only, and had refused to confess God before men, often hostile, murderous men, the gospel would have never spread beyond Jerusalem. So *confess Christ before men* in church as a good beginning, and wherever God leads. It will strengthen your faith tremendously.

3. Attend Church Faithfully

"Not forsaking the assembling of ourselves together, as the manner of some is, but exhorting one another; and so much the more, as ye see the day approaching" (Hebrews 10:25).

"Assembly" and "church" have virtually the same meaning in this context, so God is saying not to forsake the "churching" of ourselves together. *The New Testament knows nothing of a true Christian living in isolation from the local church.* We immediately become part of the body of Christ upon our salvation. Each of us have gifts to share with one another; we form different but essential parts of the body of Christ. We attend church both to give and receive. God gave godly men with special gifts to serve the church, officers called pastors to oversee and feed us, and also deacons. He carefully created the church and gave special ordinances to the church, Baptism and the Lord's Supper. He is not about to ignore His beloved church, and meet with some disobedient Christian gone A.W.O.L. Frankly, to despise the local church is to despise the Lord of the local church, whether one is aware of it or not. The Bible says that Christ is the head of the church, and the church is His body. Just as it would be nonsense to marry a person's head and have nothing to do with their body, so it would be nonsense to "marry" Christ (be joined to Him eternally through conversion), and have nothing to do with His body, the church. It is true there are sometimes hypocrites in the church, but that only proves the Bible true, for Christ predicted such in His parable of the tares and wheat. He will tend to that in due time.

The thrilling thing is that you are now a part of the family of God, filled with brothers and sisters with whom you will spend eternity! Sharing their joys and burdens, being discipled to be more and more like Jesus Christ, to His glory!

So, attend church faithfully! This is one of the surest evidences that you have truly been saved. "We know that we have passed from death unto life, because we love the brethren" (1 John 3:14). If we love Jesus and the brethren we will be delighted to be with them in church.

Be sure to find a church that clearly believes the Bible, and the Bible only, to be the inspired, infallible Word of God. Find a church that believes that Jesus Christ's blood cleanses from sin and that salvation is solely by faith in Him.

4. Read the Bible Daily

"As newborn babes, desire the sincere milk of the Word, that ye may grow thereby" (1 Peter 2:2).

As food nourishes you physically, so the Word of God is now your spiritual food. Ask God to help you understand each time you read it, and He will. Start with the gospel of John, then read 1 John, then the New Testament, and then the Old Testament. God's Word gives growth, strength, helps you to avoid sin (Psalm 119:11), illuminates your daily walk with God, brings peace, knowledge and wisdom, heightens joy, and lessens the danger of stumbling in the Christian walk (Joshua 1:8; Psalm 1:2; Colossians 3:16-17). If possible, it is best to read your Bible and pray early in the morning before facing the day, just as it is best to tune your instruments before playing in the orchestra; but any time is acceptable. It has well been said, "This book will keep you from sin, or sin will keep you from this book." *Memorize special verses!* (See also 2 Timothy 2:15.)

5. Pray Daily . . . and More Often!

"Pray without ceasing" (1 Thessalonians 5:17).

You now have a hot-line to heaven through the Lord Jesus Christ. God *promises* to answer prayer (Jeremiah 33:3; Matthew 18:19; 21:22; 1 John 5:14-15). Reading the Bible is God talking to you, prayer is you talking to God (although He speaks to your heart as you pray also) and witnessing is you talking for God. Praise God, worship Him, thank Him, and ask Him for your needs believingly every day. It is very important to tell the Lord Jesus Christ, preferably out loud, every day, that you love Him and thank Him for dying on the cross for you and giving you eternal life. It is amazing what this will do for you, in warmth, love, and abiding fellowship. It turns your mountains into molehills!

Together, prayer and Bible study form the essence of our communication with Jesus. Love in its practical application is spelled T-I-M-E. The quintessence of our love for God is expressed and enhanced by the time we spend with Him in prayer and Bible study. Those who profess to have no time for prayer and Bible study may call into question the reality of their relationship with Jesus Christ. A person claiming that he has no time for Bible study, prayer, and to live for God, is like a bird declaring that it doesn't have time to fly, or a fish claiming it has no time to swim. They were created to do these things. To love God, spend time with Him, get to really know Him and serve Him—for this we were created. At the very least, neglect insures leanness of soul, defeat and heartbreak instead of triumph and joy. Through prayer and Bible study we tap God's love and power, and grow into mature Christians established in doctrine and practice and most of all

Christlikeness. The fruit of the Spirit—love, joy, peace, longsuffering, gentleness, goodness, faith, meekness, temperance—will flow from us to His glory and attract others to Him! (Galatians 5:22, 23). Besides, what a thrill it is to see the God of the universe answering your prayers.

It is probably true that no Christian is any stronger, better, or greater, than his prayer life! It is doubtful if anything worthwhile has ever been accomplished except by prayer . . . often much prayer. Even as a new babe in Christ, like the first call of a baby to its mother, your prayers are very precious to God. Begin the habit of prayer and Bible study right now. Perhaps the greatest reward of all is that as you daily focus in on Christ through prayer and Bible study you become like Him! (2 Corinthians 3:18). As a plant looks to the sun and is transformed by photosynthesis, so let us look to Jesus in prayer and Bible study, and we will be transformed into His likeness by "Christosynthesis." Christ now actually dwells in you and intercedes for you! Pray in confidence and boldness in His name.

6. Confess Sin Instantly, Honestly, and Avoid It!

"He that covereth his sins shall not prosper, but whosoever confesseth and forsaketh them shall have mercy" (Proverbs 28:13).

Christians can still sin. Although we have a new nature, we still have the old basic, human sin nature, but God has made provision in Christ. "If we confess our sins, he is faithful and just to forgive us our sins, and to cleanse us from all unrighteousness" (1 John 1:9). Instant confession, of the thought before the deed is done, avoids much sorrow and heartbreak. But thought or deed should be confessed to God for instant forgiveness and virtually unbroken fellowship. We turn by His strength from that which caused us to stumble. Remember, a Christian can sin, but a true Christian cannot live in sin. This is true for several reasons.

First, when we came to Christ we repented of our sins (changed our minds about sin, self and the Savior) turning from self and sin as the lord of our life. "That if thou shalt confess with thy mouth the Lord Jesus (literally, *Jesus as Lord),* and shalt believe in thine heart that God hath raised Him from the dead, thou shalt be saved" (Romans 10:9).

Secondly, though we are sometimes surprised by sin, 1 John 3:9 tells us, "Whosoever is born of God doth not commit (habitually practice or continue in) sin." To illustrate, a pig and a sheep could be taken, washed, perfumed, be-ribboned, petted and kept in one's home. But if someone left the door open, the pig would head for the first mudhole and wallow happily in it; that is the pig nature. The sheep might fall into the same mudhole (I've seen some very dirty sheep), but would get out as quickly as possible. It is not a sheep's nature to wallow happily in a mudhole. So it is with the true Christian. He can never again wallow happily in sin, and will seek to flee from temptation and avoid sin, even though he can still sin.

Thirdly, we are told, "Love not the world (not speaking of trees, birds, etc. but the wicked world system presided over by Satan), neither the things that are in the world. If any man love the world, the love of the Father is not in him" (1 John 2:15). Sin and the world are what Jesus saved us from. The Bible says we have passed "from death to life," and these are the things of death. Nevertheless, when we do sin, instant confession and instant forgiveness are the answer. Sonship can never be broken; fellowship can, and sin breaks fellowship between us and God. Agreeing with God about our sin honestly in instant confession restores that sweet fellowship. (See God's promise in 1 Corinthians 10:13!)

7. Share Christ... Witness... Win the Lost

"But ye shall receive power, after that the Holy Ghost is come

upon you; and ye shall be witnesses unto me both in Jerusalem, and in all Judaea, and in Samaria, and unto the uttermost part of the earth'' (Acts 1:8).

Matthew 4:19 tells us "And He saith unto them, 'Follow me, and I will make you fishers of men.'" (Those not fishing, call into question the reality of their following.) We are saved to be conformed to the image of Christ, to bring glory to Him. However, the very heart of this is sharing Christ and winning others to Him.

Purpose: "... henceforth thou shalt catch men" (Luke 5:10b). (Actually, win them, not just fish for them.)

Promise: "He that goeth forth and weepeth, bearing precious seed, shall doubtless come again rejoicing, bringing his sheaves (the harvest, souls) with him (Psalm 126:6). "The fruit of the righteous is a tree of life; and he that winneth souls is wise" (Prov. 11:30; see also Daniel 12:3; Ezekiel 33:8.)

Priority: "For the Son of man is come to seek and to save that which was lost" (Luke 19:10). His priority and purpose now becomes our priority and purpose! "Then said Jesus to them again, 'Peace be unto you: As my Father hath sent Me, even so send I you'" (John 20:21). May we also, by His loving grace, be consumed like Paul with a passion for the lost. Paul's great heaviness and continual heart sorrow caused him to cry out, "For I could wish that myself were accursed from Christ for my brethren, my kinsmen according to the flesh" (Romans 9:3).

Winning souls! This is the one thing we can do to make Jesus and the angels of Heaven rejoice (Luke 15:9-10). There is also the rejoicing in the hearts of those reached for Christ, and the rejoicing in our own hearts and in the church.

God's command and Christ's love within compel us to witness and win souls to our Savior. Also, more souls being saved and more people being conformed to His image brings *more glory to Him.* Other motives include the joy of sharing the good news, seeing messed-up lives transformed and made abundant here and now in this life, the desire to share heaven with as many as possible, the growth and joy that occur in oneself as we witness and share Him, the demonstration of the power and compassion of Christ, and above all *saving precious souls from the awful Lake of Fire!* Truly, if salvation is the most important thing ever to happen to us, and it is, and if we "love our neighbors as ourselves" as God commands, then love constrains us to share Christ with them to deliver them from sin and Hell. This is the most wonderful privilege and purpose known to man—sharing Christ, and winning the lost to glorify Him forever.

Begin by sharing what Christ has done for you and tell those to whom you witness how it can happen to them. Share the Bible verses that brought you to salvation and assurance in Christ. You will become more and more effective as you revel in His love, learn His word, and share Him more and more with others.

8. Let Jesus Live His Life Through You

"But thanks be to God which giveth us the victory through our Lord Jesus Christ" (1 Corinthians 15:57).

We cannot live the Christian life in our strength. Christ clearly said, "without Me ye can do nothing," but we can live it in *His* strength. Letting Jesus daily live His life through you, being filled and controlled by His Holy Spirit (Ephesians 5:18) takes much of the strain out of the Christian life. Thus we can consider ourselves to be "dead indeed unto sin, but alive unto God through Jesus Christ our Lord" (Romans 6:11). And we can "walk in the Spirit, and ye shall not fulfill the lust of the flesh" (Galatians 5:16). We are not to live by *feelings* but by *faith,* and as we step out trusting in God's Word, feelings or not, we will find His Word true, His presence real, and the feelings ultimately will follow, as the *fruit* never the *root* of the Christian life. Now that you are His, bought by His blood, you will want to give Him, cheerfully and willingly, *first,* yourself, *followed* by your time, talents and treasure. Love is the compelling motive in the Christian life, not legalism, which can be a slavish, mechanical obedience to stated laws out of fear or force, bringing constraint and unhappiness.

Thus a young wife could obey a list of rules posted daily by her husband. Yet love, a higher motive, would cause the young wife to seek ways to please her husband, rules or no rules. Something he expressed that she knew would please him would bring a joyous response. This response would be done in complete freedom and bring happiness and peace. So it is with the Christian and Christ. Obeying is not legalism. It is the *attitude,* the motive, toward rules, toward obedience, which determines whether it is legalism or love-obedience. The grace of God will cause us to love and obey Jesus.

This is what the true grace of God, the unmerited favor, the free flow of His marvelous love on undeserving sinners really does. "For the grace of God that brings salvation has appeared to all men. It teaches us to say 'No' to ungodliness and worldly passions, and to live self-controlled, upright and godly lives in this present age, while we wait for the blessed hope—the glorious appearing of our great God and Savior, Jesus Christ, who gave himself for us to redeem us from all wickedness and to purify for himself a people that are his very own, eager to do what is good" (Titus 2:11-14, NIV).

Beloved, when you met Jesus, you met the Living God, for He IS God. He is risen bodily. He is alive, and He is God (John 20:28; 1 Timothy 3:16). He is now your life (Colossians 3:1-4). He can meet all your needs (Phil. 4:13, 19; 1 Peter 5:7; John 14:1-3, 27).

The shimmering splendor of His life—new life, eternal life—is yours forever! Love Jesus, love His people, love the Word, and love the lost for Him! God bless you! 1 John 5:13.

Last Words in His Love

Many people have found their lives gloriously transformed by Christ. He has fulfilled their deepest needs, calmed their fears, curbed their restlessness, taken away their guilt, lifted their burdens, given them His sweet and abiding peace. Their life is full and abundant, they revel in His love, they enjoy the Christian life, and love other Christians. Jesus is all in all to them, His life is now their life, and they love it.

Unfortunately, many others, though they say the same things about Jesus, and claim they know Him and love Him, are still wallowing most of the time in defeat and discouragement. They are still restless, unfulfilled, often swallowed up in troubles, bad habits, sin, self-pity. They are barely able to keep their heads above water in the Christian life, much less bring any glory to Christ, grow, mature and be faithful as Christians, lead others to Christ, or be real pillars in the church.

Some, of course, have never been truly saved, profession or not. However, many others are like a person who goes to the doctor, gets a prescription with eight ingredients in it, and scratches out one or several of the ingredients before he gives it to the druggist to be filled. Then, after less than desirable or even disastrous results, he blames the doctor or the druggist for the medicine not working. He may even lose faith in the doctor, or claim he is a fraud. Tragically, some do this in the Christian life. We must do what the Great Physician prescribes to enjoy and grow successfully in the Christian life. Love, loving Jesus, is the bottom line, but we must not take lightly 2 John 6a: "And this is love, that we walk after his commandments."

You may find these following scriptural principles helpful:
1. Victory is basically a gift, just as salvation was (2 Corinthi-

ans 15:57).

2. Know that you are dead to sin (Romans 6:11). Sin is not dead to you! You are, however, alive to God! (Ephesians 2:1).

3. Yield yourself to Jesus as one alive from the dead (Romans 12:1-2).

4. Believe, accept, reckon, rely on, claim, and live these facts by faith not feelings.

5. This is all true because of your identification with Christ in His death, burial and resurrection.

6. Claim His control, the filling of His Holy Spirit, by faith (Galatians 5:16; 2:20).

We must exercise the power of the Holy Spirit in our lives by faith. While *He* provides the power *we* do it by faith that He is working in and through us. As Charles Ryrie well said, "God's working is not suspended because I work; neither is God's working always apart from my working."

Perhaps the greatest secret of that new life is to really belive and claim Romans 8:28 and to *show that* confidence in Christ constantly. How? Practice always the following verses by faith, not feeling—for all things "good" and "bad:"

> "And we know that all things work together for good to them that love God, to them who are the called according to his purpose" (Romans 8:28).

> "In everything give thanks, for this is the will of God in Christ Jesus concerning you" (1 Thessalonians 5:18).

Another tremendous, life-changing truth is that God sees us as perfected forever in Jesus Christ! This is our *position* in Christ. "For by one offering he hath perfected forever them that are sanctified (saved)" (Hebrews 10:14).

Claim this truth, rejoice in it, and your *practice* will begin to reflect your *position* as a true child of God! May God bless you in your new life!

Bible Study Questions

The following Bible studies have been prepared to help the reader better understand and apply the principles presented in this book. Please take the time to go through each of the nine short studies and read the Scripture passages provided.

If you have further questions about salvation and the Christian life, you are invited to contact the publisher of this book: *Institute for Religious Research, 1340 Monroe NW, Grand Rapids, MI 49505 U.S.A. (616)451-4562.*

Study No. 1 — Who is Jesus Christ? (pages 11-31)

1. Is Jesus Christ God? Pages 11-31. Give proofs. ....
   ....
   ....
   Was He always God? .... Isaiah 9:6; John 8:28; Philippians 2:5-8; Compare Isaiah 6:1-10 with John 12:35-41. Who did Isaiah really see when he saw the Lord? ....
2. Is Jesus Christ the Creator of the world? ....
   Compare Genesis 1:1 & John 1:1-3, 14.
3. Was Jesus worshipped as God? .... Compare Exodus 3:14 & John 8:58; also Exodus 34:14 & John 20:28, Matthew 28:9.
   Who does Exodus 34:14 say should be worshipped? ....
4. The same exclusive titles, names and attributes given to God the Father, are also given to Jesus. Isaiah 43:10, Deuteronomy 6:4, Isaiah 45:21, and Isaiah 46:9-10, declare that there is only *one* God! Yet God the Father, in the Old Testament, and God the Son, in the New Testament are called *The* Creator, *The* First and Last, *The* Shepherd, *The* Saviour, *The* one true GOD, *The* Lord, etc.! How does Philippians 2:5-11 fulfill Isaiah 9:6?
   ....
   Who is *The Almighty God*? .... Genesis 1:17; Revelation 1:5-8.
   The Holy Spirit is also .... Acts 5:3-4; Luke 1:35.
   There are 3 persons in the One True God: God the Father, God the Son, and God the Holy Spirit. True or False? ....
5. Jesus said that those who saw Him had seen the Father (John 14:9). Compare Isaiah 44:6 with Revelation 1:8, 11, 17. See Genesis 1:1 & John 1:1-3; Compare Psalm 23:1 & John 10:11. Luke 1:47-2:11. These verses

clearly declare that Jesus Christ is .... When was God manifest in the flesh? .... 1 Timothy 3:16.
6. Who forgives sin? .... Mark 2:7-11; Colossians 1:14.
7. Did Jesus Christ rise bodily from the tomb? .... Luke 24:1-7. What did this prove? .... Romans 1:3-4 Is the evidence solid? ...... Pgs. 13-19; Acts 1:1-3. Give at least five proofs.
....
....
....

What else did the resurrection of Christ accomplish? 1 Corinthians 15:51-58; Romans 4:25; Hebrews 7:25; Acts 1:8-11. List. ....
....
....

Why did Jesus Christ perform miracles? ....
.... (John 20:29-31)
8. Who alone can save us? .... (John 14:6; Acts 4:12). Who alone is coming back from heaven to take Christians to their forever home? .... (Acts 1:11; John 14:1-3; 1 Thessalonians 4:13-18; Titus 2:13)
9. Who alone is our Lord and our God? .... (John 20:28) [This study about Jesus Christ is so vital, at least two, one hour sessions, should be spent on it. All scriptures should be looked up and read. The answers should be carefully checked.]

Study No. 2 — Baptism (pages 43-44)

1. What washes away sin? 1 John 1:7. "... and the .... of Jesus Christ his Son cleanseth us from all sin. Romans 5:8-9; Hebrews 10:19; Revelation 5:9 and 1:5, "... Unto him that loved us and washed us from our sins in his own ...."
2. Either the blood of Jesus or water baptism washes away our sins. Which is it? (1 Peter 3:21; Ephesians 2:8-9). ....
3. There *is* a baptism that occurs simultaneously with salvation, but it has nothing to do with water. 1 Corinthians 12:13, "For by one Spirit are we all baptized into one body..." Water baptism only pictures this — True or

False? .... At salvation, we are thus placed in Christ, and become .... in Christ, according to 2 Corinthians 5:17.
4. We are saved by faith in Jesus before being baptized. Acts 2:41; 8:35-38; 16:31; Luke 7:50; 18:13-14. All of these were saved before water baptism. True or False? .... The thief on the cross was saved, and taken to heaven without water baptism (Luke 23:39-43). True or False? ...... In clear detail Acts 10 shows that Cornelius and the Gentiles in his house believed, received the .... of the ...., magnified God and *then* as new believers, Christians, were baptized in .... See Acts 10:43-47.
5. Baptism is done to obey and follow Jesus. It is not optional. Baptism pictures on the outside what Christ has done on the inside, and publicly identifies us with Jesus Christ in his death, burial and resurrection. It testifies to our death to the old life with Him, our burial with Him, and our resurrection to the new life with Jesus Christ. Romans 6:1-5. "... planted together in the .... of his death, we shall be also in the .... of his ...."
What does John 14:23 teach about obedience? ....
....

Study No. 3 — Confess Christ Before Men (pages 44-45)
1. According to Romans 10:9-10, we must .... with our .... what we believe in our heart about Jesus, for our decision to be valid.
2. According to Luke 12:8-9, if we do not confess Jesus before men, He will not confess us as His! He will .... us before the angels of God!
3. We believe in our heart unto righteousness, as Romans 10:9-10 states, and confession confirms that decision. True or False? .... Many were martyred, tortured, burned at the stake for Jesus, but they would not keep their mouth shut about Him ... neither should we!

Study No. 4 — Attend Church Faithfully! (pages 45-46)
1. "Not forsaking the .... of ourselves together ..." Hebrews 10:25. This is a direct command of God to attend ....

2. Matthew 13:24-30. If there were no tares (hypocrites) in the church, the .... would not be true!
3. People without Christ are .... in their trespasses and sins. Christians have been made .... in Christ. (Ephesians 2:1-2). It would be a strange person indeed who preferred the company of rotting corpses, of dead people, to the company of living people! One powerful reason that we go to church is because we .... the .... (1 John 3:14).
4. 1 Corinthians 12, Romans 12 and Ephesians 4, declare that God has given .... to every Christian and gifted men to the church, Pastors and Deacons. He has given ordinances to the church to be observed — Baptism and the Lord's Supper. He has commissioned His church to be an evangelistic/missionary outreach to a lost world. Will He then ignore what He instituted to meet with some A.W.O.L. professing Christian who has a 'better' idea and scorns the church? Yes or No? ....
5. Since Christ is the Head, and the Church is His body, can we then 'marry,' be joined to the Head, and have nothing to do with the Body? Yes or No? .... (Ephesians 5:25, 31-32)
6. God asks that we give to Him our tithes (tenth) and offerings through the local church. To give lovingly and lavishly to Him who shed His blood for us is no burden to the obedient Christian. The widow was commended for giving all she had (Luke 21:1-4).

He will take care of us and provide our true needs! Philippians 4:19; Matthew 6:24-33. His instructions for giving — 2 Corinthians 9:6-7. Notice that God says we should not give ...., "for God loveth a .... giver." It is also an investment for eternity. God says, "For where your treasure is, there will your .... be also" (Matthew 6:21).

Study No. 5 — Read the Bible Daily (page 46)

1. New Christians need the .... of the Word of God. 1 Peter 2:2.
2. More mature Christians need the .... of the Word of God (Hebrews 5:12; I Corinthians 3:2). Who can understand the Bible? ....(1 Corinthians 2:14-16) Why? ....
....

The Christ Changed Life

3. Reading the Bible is to our spiritual life, what eating .... is to our physical life.
4. We are .... by the Word of God (1 Peter 1:23). The Word of God is likened unto ....
5. .... cometh by hearing, and hearing by the .... of .... (Romans 10:17).
6. The Word of God is .... and ...., according to Hebrews 4:12, and is a discerner of the .... and .... of the heart.
7. We hide God's Word in our hearts that we might not .... against Him, according to Psalm 119:11. His Word will also .... our way, according to Psalm 119:9. In this dark world, His word is a .... unto our feet and a .... unto our path, according to Psalm 119:105.
8. We are to .... day and night in the law (Word of God) states Psalm 1:2. Joshua 1:8 tells us to ...... all that is .... therein.
9. We are *especially* to .... and to .... the word of truth, according to 2 Timothy 2:15.

Study No. 6. — Pray Daily ... and More Often!
(pages 47, 48)

1. In 1 Thessalonians 5:17, we are told to pray without ....
2. God did not spare His own Son, His greatest gift, in order to reach us. Having given us His greatest gift, He now assures us he will freely ..... us .... Romans 8:32.
3. Prayer involves praise, confession, adoration, asking, thanking, supplication, communication, etc. but basically is just .... to our Father.
4. Jeremiah 33:3 tells us to "........ unto me, (God), and I *will* answer thee, and shew thee .... and .... things which thou knowest not."
5. Matthew 21:22, asserts that the key in having our prayers answered is .... Our prayers should be .... (James 5:16)
6. Some hindrances to answered prayer are found in Psalm 66:18; Hebrews 11:6; James 1:6-8; and James 4:2-3. List them. ....
....
....
....

7. Since Jesus is our high priest, praying for us, we come boldly in His righteousness to the .... of .... Hebrews 4:14-16. We can obtain .... and find .... to help in time of need.
8. The Holy Spirit also makes .... for us. Romans 8:26. Finally, 1 John 5:14-15, tells us that, "... this is the confidence that we have in him, that, if we ask anything .... to .... he heareth us: And if we know that he .... us, whatsoever we ask, we know we .... the petitions that we desired of him."

Study No. 7 — Confess Sin Instantly and Forsake it!
(pages 48-49)

Christians can still sin, but a true Christian cannot live in sin. 1 John 3:9, "Whosoever is born of God doth not commit (practice) sin;..."

1. Proverbs 28:13 is both pithy and pointed, "He that .... his .... shall not ...., but he that .... and .... them shall have ...."
2. 1 John 1:9 tells us what to do immediately when we sin in thought, word or deed, "If we confess our sins, he is faithful and just to .... our sins, and to .... us from *all* ...." In the pig and sheep illustration given on page 49, what does the pig do and why, in regard to the mudhole, and what does the sheep do and why, in regard to the mudhole? How does this apply to the Christian?
....
....
3. When we sin as Christians, *fellowship* with God is broken, but *sonship* is forever, and cannot be broken. When we were born into God's family, He promised us that He will always make a way to .... when we are tempted (1 Corinthians 10:13; 2 Timothy 2:22).
4. When we confess our sins as Christians, we must believe what God has said in 1 John 1:9, that He has .... us! Not to forgive ourselves, when God has forgiven us, is to act as if we are holier than God!

Study No. 8 — Share Christ to Win the Lost!
(pages 49-51)

1. In Matthew 4:19, Jesus said, ". . . Follow me, and I will make you .... of men." Are those not .... truly following Jesus? (Acts 1:8)

2. Proverbs 11:30 says, "The fruit of the righteous is a tree of life; and he that winneth souls is wise." Since God wants *all* Christians to be wise, He wants all Christians to be .... winners.

3. Daniel 12:3: "And they that be *wise* shall shine as the brightness of the firmament; and they that turn many to righteousness *as the* .... forever and ever."

4. Ezekiel 33:8 says, "When I say to the wicked, O wicked man, thou shalt surely die; if thou dost not .... to .... the wicked from his way, that wicked man shall die in his iniquity; but his blood will I require at thine hand." (also verse 9!).

5. God's promise is for every Christian. "He that .... forth and ...., bearing precious seed, shall *doubtless* come again with rejoicing, bringing his sheaves with him" (Psalm 126:6).

6. Is soul winning urgent? .... (John 4:35; Acts 20:20, 21, 31).

7. Luke 19:10 declares, the *purpose* for which Jesus came to earth, lived among men, and died the horrible, bloody death on the cross. "For the Son of man is come to seek and save that which was lost."

8. His command in John 20:21 is equally clear, ". . . as my Father hath sent me, even so send I you." What then is *our* purpose? ....

9. Jesus said in Luke 5:10b, ". . . from henceforth thou shalt *catch* men." Not just fish for them. He does not just tell us to fish and be indifferent as to whether or not we catch any fish! If I turn a faucet on and no water comes I don't just shrug and say, "O well, I've been faithful, I turned the faucet on . . . it must be God's will that no water comes!" I do my best to find out *why* no water comes, and find the problem and the solution. If I am not winning souls, even though I am 'witnessing,' I want to to find out why and remedy the situation. God is not willing that *any* should perish! He wants all Christians to win souls. Let Jesus love lost souls through you, involving you in His love for the lost!

Study No. 9 — Let Jesus Live His Life Through You!
(pages 51-54)

Real Christians *will have* a changed life, (see 2 Corinthians 5:17, 1 John 2:4; 1 John 3:6-14.) This change is accomplished by the indwelling Christ (Romans 12:1,2).

1. Live by faith, not feeling! Faith is the *root*, feeling is the *fruit*. We do not have to 'feel' the presence of God to know He is with us. His promise is enough! Matthew 28:20, "... and, lo, *I am with you alway*, even unto the end of the world. Amen." The truth of the presence of the Lord Jesus Christ dwelling in believers and being with them always, in no way depends on feeling! Fact, Faith and Feelings are usually in that order.
2. Jesus said, in John 15:5, "... for without me ye can do ...."
3. Romans 6:11 tells us, "Likewise reckon ye also yourselves to be .... indeed to sin, but .... to God through Jesus Christ our Lord."
4. Before we were saved we were self-centered, managers and 'gods' of our own life, as Isaiah 53:6 says, describing the very heart of sin, "we have turned every one to his own way," and then says of this very sin, "... the Lord hath .... on him the .... of us all."
5. Who is to be the Christian's Lord, Master, owner, boss, God? .... Romans 10:9-10. Luke 6:46 shows the futility of profession without possession, and incidentally what 'Lord' means in this context! "And why call ye me, Lord, Lord, and .... the things which I say?"
6. For victory in the Christian life there must be commitment to Christ. This involves letting Jesus daily live His life through you being .... by His Holy Spirit, Ephesians 5:18. This results in bearing the fruit of the Holy Spirit, Galatians 5:22-23. Name them! We are told in Galatians 5:16 to ".............. in the ...., and ye *shall not* fulfill the .... of the ...."
7. Who should we be expecting, 1 Thessalonians 4:13-18, ..., and what effect will this anticipation have on our life? .... (1 John 3:1-3).

The Christ Changed Life — 63

8. In James 1:2, we are told to "... count it all *joy* when we fall into divers temptations" (testings, trials.) This is possible because we understand that Romans 8:28 is *true*, not that all things are good, in themselves, but God is working *in all* things for good, to those of us who love Him! Thus, "All things work together for .... to them that .... God!" 1 Thessalonians 5:18, "In everything give thanks: for this is the .... of .... in Christ Jesus concerning you." We can always begin by thanking Him that He loves us, that He shed His blood on the cross for us, that He saved us from sin and Hell, and that the sufferings of this present time are not worth being compared with the glory He has prepared for us forever! List the verse in Romans 8 that says this ....

9. Sum up the six points for a victorious Christian life given on pages 53-54, of *The Compelling Christ*. ....
   ....
   ....
   ....

Rejoice daily in Jesus and His salvation!

If you have read the book, *The Compelling Christ*, carefully, and prayed to receive Christ, and still are not sure you are saved, consider the following very carefully:

1. Study the elevator illustration on pages 39-40 until you understand it. You still may be relying on 'feelings' rather than trusting Jesus by faith and believing God's Word that He has saved you, if you *believed Him*!
2. Many people pray and ask Jesus to save them, and do not get saved. One very common reason is that they do not believe He has saved them when they asked Him to. When we ask Jesus to save us, *we must believe Him that He did*! 1 John 5:9-13 makes it very clear.

Finally, beloved, this little book has been written with much prayer and concern that you might know what being a Christian and living the Christian life really involves. In Jesus' day many who started with Him quit (John 6:66-71). But when Jesus asked the Twelve if they would also go away, Peter

poignantly cried, "Lord, to whom shall we go? Thou hast the words of eternal life." The Bible says, according to the "Living Letters" paraphrase in 1 John 2:4:
"Someone may say, 'I am a Christian, I am on my way to Heaven, I belong to Christ.' But if he doesn't do what Christ tells him to, he is a liar."

And, in John 3:6-10:
"So if we stay close to Him, obedient to Him, we won't be sinning either; but those who keep on sinning should realize this: they sin because they have never really known Him and become His. Oh, dear people, don't let anyone deceive you about this: if you are constantly doing what is good, it is because you are good, even as He is. But if you keep sinning, it shows you that you belong to Satan, who since he first began to sin has kept steadily at it. But the Son of God came to destroy these works of the devil. The person who has been born into God's family does not make a practice of sinning because now God's life is in him, and so he can't keep on sinning, for this new life has been born into him and controls him — he has been born again. So now we can tell who is a child of God and who belongs to Satan. Whoever is living a life of sin and doesn't love his brother shows that he is not in God's family." *(Note: Although the King James Version is clear, we have used the "Living Letters" here as a vivid commentary.)*

Pretty clear, isn't it? This explains why many who start the Christian life, later quit. They make a decision for Christ and then refuse to follow Him. 2 Peter 2:20 is a terrible warning about this, but 1 John 2:19 declares:
"They went out from us, but they were not of us; for if they had been of us, they would no doubt have continued with us: but they went out, that they might be made manifest that they were not all of us."

God plainly says real disciples will continue, and He cannot lie. False ones, sooner or later, will find reasons or excuses for dropping out. But not so those who know they have been saved, have met the Risen Christ, have had their life and purpose transformed by Him. Hebrews 6:9 says, "But, beloved, we are persuaded better things of you, and things that accompany salvation, though we thus speak." Practice 1 Thessalonians 5:18 because of Romans 8:28 for victory, outreach and the glory of God!